I0407585

THE TOILET BOOK

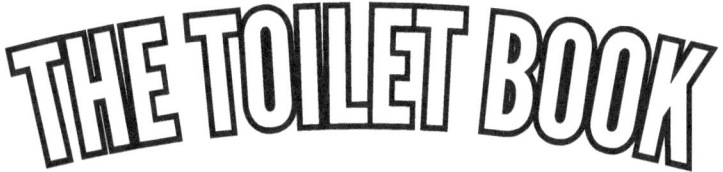

MOVIE HISTORY

LIGHTS, CAMERA, ANECDOTES!

by
Herman Cooper

Copyright © 2023 by Herman Cooper

All rights reserved. No part of this publication may be reproduced, distributed, or transmitted in any form or by any means, including photocopying, recording, or other electronic or mechanical methods, without the prior written permission of the publisher, except in the case of brief quotations embodied in critical reviews and certain other noncommercial uses permitted by copyright law.

ISBN: 9798861180429

Cover Design by: Herman Cooper

Disclaimer:

While every effort has been made to ensure the accuracy and reliability of the information contained in this book, it is intended for entertainment purposes only. There may be occasional discrepancies or omissions in the content. Neither the author nor the publisher assumes any responsibility or liability for any errors or oversights, or for the use or interpretation of the information contained in this book. For more detailed or comprehensive information, readers are encouraged to consult specialized sources or experts in the field.

www.thetoiletbooks.com

Flush
Fiction &
Facts

"Every great film should seem new every time you see it."– Roger Ebert

Famous Bathroom Scenes

"Psycho" (1960) - Perhaps the most iconic bathroom scene in film history, Alfred Hitchcock's "Psycho" features the chilling shower murder of Marion Crane by Norman Bates.

"The Shining" (1980) - The infamous scene where Jack Nicholson's character utters the line, "Here's Johnny!" while breaking through a bathroom door with an ax.

"Pulp Fiction" (1994) - John Travolta's character, Vincent Vega, has a few critical moments in the restroom, but the most significant one leads to an unexpected and deadly confrontation upon his exit.

"There's Something About Mary" (1998) - Ben Stiller's character gets into a painfully embarrassing situation involving a zipper while preparing for his date with Mary.

The Big Lebowski" (1998) - The Dude (Jeff Bridges) is attacked in his own home and ends up with his head in the toilet, courtesy of some inept henchmen.

"Dumb and Dumber" (1994) - Jeff Daniels' character, Harry, suffers from a severe case of food poisoning, leading to an uproariously comical scene in a bathroom.

"Bridesmaids" (2011) - After dining at a dubious restaurant, the bridesmaids find themselves racing to a fancy bridal shop bathroom with dire results.

Trainspotting" (1996) - Ewan McGregor's character, Renton, plunges into the "worst toilet in Scotland" in a surreal scene, diving deep into the filth to retrieve some lost opium suppositories.

"Lethal Weapon 2" (1989) - Detective Murtaugh (Danny Glover) finds himself stuck on a bomb-rigged toilet, leading to a tense yet comically handled situation.

THE TOILET BOOK
MOVIE HISTORY

From the silent eras' dramatic shadows to the CGI spectacles of today, cinema has seen revolutions, evolutions, and every twist in between. And while our lavatory experiences might not be as illustrious, they're just as filled with... drama? Well, let's not go down that drain.

Each chapter of this book offers a quick glimpse—a 'scene,' if you will—into the world of films. And trust us, whether you're in for a quick commercial break or an epic saga, there's a tidbit for every time frame.

After all, where better to relive the history of cinema than in the one place where you can truly escape, uninterrupted (we hope) for a few minutes?

So, the next time you reach for that roll, remember: much like a good film, this book promises entertainment, education, and a perfect way to pass... time.

Sit back (or down), relax, and let the show begin!

CHAPTER

ONE:

THE BIRTH OF CINEMA
(LATE 1800s - EARLY 1900s)

THE DAWN OF A NEW ART FORM

As the 19th century came to a close and the world stood on the brink of the 20th, a revolution was quietly brewing in the world of entertainment. Far removed from the confines of stages and theaters, a novel medium emerged, harnessing the marvels of technology to captivate audiences.

This was the dawn of cinema.

From modest devices that allowed a single viewer to catch a fleeting glimpse of movement to the grandeur of early movie theaters, the origins of cinema are imbued with innovation, experimentation, and a touch of magic. The motion picture, as it was fondly called, promised not just a new form of entertainment, but a new way of seeing the world, of sharing stories, and of dreaming dreams.

Imagine the wonder in the eyes of the audience witnessing moving pictures for the first time – trains rushing towards them, fantastical trips to the moon, and the earliest narratives played out in silent symphony on the screen. This chapter embarks on a journey through those pioneering days, when inventors, artists, and audiences alike stood at the cusp of a cinematic universe waiting to be explored.

So, sit back, dim the lights, and let's rewind to a time when the magic of cinema was just beginning to flicker to life.

Roundhay's Record

The first film ever, "Roundhay Garden Scene" (1888), lasted just about 2 seconds. Shot in a garden in Leeds, England, it's a testament to the novelty and constraints of early film.

Edison's Vision

Thomas Edison's kinetoscope, introduced in 1894, allowed one person at a time to view moving pictures. This personal viewing experience marked the first commercial step towards cinema.

Lumière Brothers' Legacy

The Lumière brothers held the first commercial public screening using their invention, the Cinématographe, in 1895. This event in Paris is where the public cinema experience truly began.

First Film Studio

Thomas Edison's Black Maria studio, founded in 1893 in New Jersey, is considered the first ever film studio. Its quirky name comes from its resemblance to black police wagons of the time.

The Great Train Robbery

Released in 1903, "The Great Train Robbery" is credited as the first narrative film, running around 12 minutes. Its compelling narrative set the stage for future storytelling in film.

Origin of "Moviola"

The Moviola, an early film editing device, was originally invented in 1924 to allow Hollywood directors to review film footage. Its innovative design became the standard for film editing for many years.

Pioneering Sci-Fi

The 1902 film "A Trip to the Moon" by Georges Méliès is considered one of the first sci-fi movies. With groundbreaking special effects, it showcased cinema's potential for fantastical storytelling.

First Cartoon Character

The first animated cartoon character, Gertie the Dinosaur, was created by Winsor McCay in 1914. This pioneering animation set the stage for a whole new genre of film.

Color Comes into Play

The first successful color process was Technicolor, introduced in 1916, though it would take decades for color films to become mainstream. This innovation added a new dimension to visual storytelling.

First Film with Sound

Though not entirely synchronized, "Don Juan" in 1926 was the first film to use the Vitaphone sound-on-disc system. This marked the beginning of the transition from silent films to "talkies."

Box Office Beginnings

In 1905, Pittsburgh opened the first movie theater, or "nickelodeon", which charged a nickel for admission. It marked the rise of dedicated venues for film viewing.

Early Film Critic

The first film critic, Ricciotto Canudo, penned "The Birth of the Sixth Art" in 1911, arguing that cinema was a distinct art form. His advocacy positioned film alongside traditional arts.

The Invention of the Close-Up

D.W. Griffith, one of early cinema's most influential directors, is often credited for pioneering the use of the close-up shot. This technique revolutionized how emotions were conveyed on screen.

Beginnings of Bollywood

India's first silent film, "Raja Harishchandra" (1913), laid the foundation for what would become the massive Bollywood industry. This film demonstrated the universal appeal of cinema.

Birth of the Film Star

Florence Lawrence is considered the first movie star, and she was the first film actor to be named publicly in 1910. Before her, actors were often uncredited, their identities remaining a mystery to audiences.

CHAPTER TWO:

THE SILENT ERA
(1910s – LATE 1920s)

WHISPERS AND SHADOWS

In the nascent glow of the 20th century, as the world underwent rapid transformations, cinema too found its unique voice – paradoxically, in silence. The Silent Era, spanning from the 1910s to the late 1920s, was an era where emotions were conveyed not through spoken words but through expressive eyes, exaggerated actions, and intertitles that whispered the dialogues.

Imagine theaters filled with audiences gazing intently at the screen, the only sounds being the soft rustling of seats, the occasional gasp, and the melodic accompaniment of a live piano or orchestra. Stars like Charlie Chaplin, Buster Keaton, and Clara Bow didn't need words; their very presence was magnetic, speaking volumes through simple gestures and poignant expressions.

This was a time of pure cinematic artistry. Filmmakers, devoid of dialogue's crutch, relied on innovative techniques, shadows, and light to narrate their tales. The audience too played an active role, using their imaginations to complete the narrative, making it a deeply personal experience.

As we delve into this chapter, let's journey back to a time when cinema was a visual sonnet, when every frame was a painting, and every flicker told a story. Welcome to the Silent Era, where the magic of film spoke louder than words.

Chaplin's Charisma

Charlie Chaplin, with his iconic bowler hat and mustache, became the world's first international film star during the silent era. His comedic genius in films like "The Tramp" made him a global sensation.

A Sound Breakthrough

"The Jazz Singer" (1927) made cinematic history as the first "talkie," marking the decline of silent films. Audiences were astounded to hear synchronized dialogue and music for the first time.

Swanson's Spotlight

Gloria Swanson, a major silent film star, transitioned into talkies with the film "Sunset Boulevard" (1950), famously uttering, "I am big. It's the pictures that got small."

Nosferatu's Niche

The 1922 film "Nosferatu" is an unauthorized adaptation of Bram Stoker's "Dracula." Despite attempts to destroy all copies, it survived and became a defining horror classic of the silent era.

Keaton's Craft

Buster Keaton, renowned for his physical comedy and deadpan expression, performed his own death-defying stunts, making him a true pioneer in action-comedy.

The Phantom's Phenomenon

"The Phantom of the Opera" (1925) stunned audiences with Lon Chaney's groundbreaking makeup techniques. His portrayal remains one of the most iconic versions of the phantom.

Flapper Films Flourish

The Roaring Twenties brought the flapper culture to the big screen. Clara Bow, known as the "It Girl," epitomized the spirit and vivacity of the flapper era in her films.

Birth of the Oscars

In 1929, the first Academy Awards were held, honoring the best films of 1927 and 1928. "Wings" took home the award for Best Picture, a silent film testament to the era's brilliance.

Silent Star Transition

Many silent film stars struggled to transition into talkies due to various factors, from unsuitable voices to foreign accents, marking the end of several illustrious careers.

The Metropolis Marvel

Fritz Lang's "Metropolis" (1927) is hailed as one of the most influential science fiction films ever. Its futuristic visuals and social commentary continue to inspire filmmakers.

Fairbanks' Fantasy World

Douglas Fairbanks, the swashbuckling hero of silent cinema, starred in adventure classics like "The Thief of Bagdad" (1924), setting a benchmark for action films.

Valentino's Veneration

Rudolph Valentino became a heartthrob after his role in "The Sheik" (1921). His unexpected death in 1926 led to mass hysteria and a reported several suicide attempts by desolate fans.

The Rise of Film Scores

Even in silence, films weren't truly quiet. Live orchestras or organists often accompanied screenings, enhancing emotions and adding depth to the viewing experience.

Silent Diversity

Despite technological limitations, silent films experimented with color tints, imaginative title cards, and innovative camera tricks, pushing the boundaries of storytelling.

Garbo's Grace

Greta Garbo, the enigmatic Swedish star, transitioned successfully from silent films to talkies. With her sultry voice, she proclaimed in "Anna Christie" (1930), "Gimme a whiskey," signaling her sound debut.

CHAPTER

THREE:

THE GOLDEN AGE OF HOLLYWOOD (1930s - 1940s)

GLEAMING REELS AND SILVER SCREENS

As the sun painted golden hues over the Hollywood sign, a cinematic revolution was unfurling beneath. The 1930s and 1940s, often celebrated as Hollywood's Golden Age, were a period of unparalleled glamour, innovation, and cultural influence. It was an era where celluloid dreams danced vividly, every frame dripping with elegance, emotion, and exquisite artistry.

The glitz of Tinseltown wasn't merely confined to its star-studded premieres or the hallowed boulevards where legends were born. It was reflected in the very fabric of its creations. From the sweeping Technicolor vistas of "Gone with the Wind" to the shadowy alleyways of Film Noir, cinema evolved into a canvas of boundless imagination and powerful storytelling.

Yet, beneath the glossy veneer lay a world grappling with change. The specter of war, societal shifts, and evolving morals cast their shadows on the silver screen. Hollywood responded with grace, churning out tales of hope, heroism, love, and despair. Musicals, epics, thrillers, and dramas—all coalesced to define a generation and shape the very ethos of film.

An era where legends were etched in light, where every note, dance step, and dialogue echoed with magic. Welcome to the Golden Age of Hollywood, where dreams knew no bounds and cinema was truly king.

Technicolor Triumph

The 1939 classics "The Wizard of Oz" and "Gone with the Wind" were among the earliest films to fully harness the vibrant magic of Technicolor. Their vivid hues revolutionized cinematic storytelling, offering audiences an escape into worlds more colorful than their own.

Monsters and Men

Universal Pictures became the home of monsters in the 1930s, introducing iconic characters like Dracula, Frankenstein, and The Mummy. These horror staples showed the darker desires and fears of society, captivating audiences with a mix of terror and allure.

The Disney Dream

In 1937, Walt Disney released "Snow White and the Seven Dwarfs," the world's first feature-length animated film. Critics were skeptical, but its success paved the way for a new genre, forever altering the cinematic landscape.

The Hays Code

Introduced in the early '30s, the Hays Production Code set strict moral guidelines for films. While it limited explicit content, it inadvertently encouraged filmmakers to become more creative and subtle in their storytelling techniques.

Star Systems and Studios

Major studios like MGM, Warner Bros., and Paramount dominated the era with their star system, meticulously crafting and controlling the public images of their top actors, turning them into larger-than-life icons.

Bogart and Bacall

Humphrey Bogart and Lauren Bacall's electric chemistry in "To Have and Have Not" (1944) wasn't just for the screen. Their off-screen romance became one of Hollywood's most legendary love stories.

The Birth of Film Noir

The 1940s saw the emergence of film noir, a genre characterized by moody black-and-white visuals, complex plots, and morally ambiguous characters. These tales of crime and passion mirrored the societal anxieties of the time.

Oscars' Only Tie

In a unique turn of events, the 1969 Best Actress Oscar saw a tie between Katharine Hepburn and Barbra Streisand. While this event happened after the Golden Age, it remains a nod to Hollywood's rich legacy of talent.

Hitchcock's Mastery

Alfred Hitchcock, the "Master of Suspense," redefined thriller and horror genres in this era. With classics like "Psycho" and "Rear Window," he showcased the power of suspense over shock.

Rise of the Musicals

Musicals like "Meet Me in St. Louis" became synonymous with the Golden Age, combining stellar performances, catchy tunes, and intricate dance numbers to create pure cinematic joy.

Wartime Cinema

World War II greatly influenced Hollywood, from war dramas to propaganda films. Cinema became a tool for both escapism and patriotism, reflecting the era's hopes and fears.

The Femme Fatale

The Golden Age introduced the archetype of the femme fatale: mysterious, seductive women who used their charm for personal gain, often leading men to their doom in iconic noirs like "Double Indemnity."

Sweeping Epics

Films like "Casablanca" and "Ben-Hur" are testaments to the era's love for grand narratives. These epics, with their grand sets and sprawling stories, offered audiences a chance to travel to distant lands and eras.

Bette Davis' Eyes

Bette Davis, with her distinctive eyes and unmatched acting prowess, became one of the era's most celebrated actresses, setting a standard with roles that showcased strong, complex women.

The Western Wave

The rugged landscapes and moral dilemmas of Westerns like "Stagecoach" and "High Noon" captured the spirit of the American frontier, reflecting the nation's mythos and ideals.

CHAPTER FOUR:

THE RISE OF COLOR AND TECHNOLOGICAL ADVANCEMENTS (1950s)

Technicolor Dreams and Silver Screen Legends

The 1950s, a period often remembered as the golden age of conformity, bore witness to radical transformations.

As America danced to the rhythm of rock 'n' roll and watched the world through television's nascent glow, Hollywood was on the cusp of a revolution. It is a decade where technological innovations melded seamlessly with iconic performances, creating cinematic masterpieces that still resonate today.

Technicolor turned Hollywood's monochromatic dreams into colorful epics, while the early experiments with 3D and widescreen promised an escape from the humdrum of daily life.

Yet, it wasn't just technology setting the screen ablaze. Stars like Marilyn Monroe, James Dean, and Marlon Brando illuminated theaters, each bringing a distinct charisma that left audiences spellbound. Directors, not to be outdone, carved narratives that oscillated between the boundless optimism of post-war America and the lurking shadows of the Cold War.

From the enchanting fairy tales of Disney to the suspenseful masterpieces of Hitchcock, the '50s cinema was a rich mosaic of style and substance.

So, sit back and let's journey together into a decade where cinema, fueled by innovation and imagination, redefined entertainment, shaping the contours of what was to become modern filmmaking.

Dawn of Technicolor

While Technicolor was introduced earlier, it was the 1950s that truly saw its dominance. Films like "Singin' in the Rain" showcased vibrant palettes, turning black-and-white landscapes into colorful masterpieces.

Monroe's Iconic Moment

Marilyn Monroe's skirt-flying scene in "The Seven Year Itch" (1955) is legendary. While it seemed spontaneous, it was a meticulously planned shot that became one of cinema's most iconic images.

Launch of 3D Films

Hollywood tried to outshine TV by introducing 3D films. The excitement began with "Bwana Devil" in 1952, but the craze was short-lived as audiences preferred traditional viewing.

James Dean

With only three major films before his tragic death in 1955, James Dean became an enduring symbol of youthful rebellion, epitomized by his role in "Rebel Without a Cause."

Disney's Fairy Tale Era

The 1950s was golden for Disney, releasing classics like "Cinderella" (1950), "Peter Pan" (1953), and "Sleeping Beauty" (1959), enchanting children and adults alike.

Audrey Hepburn's Radiance

Audrey Hepburn graced the screen with elegance in classics like "Roman Holiday" (1953), for which she won her first Oscar, solidifying her as Hollywood's sweetheart.

Godzilla Roars to Screen

1954 saw the birth of a cinematic titan with "Godzilla". This Japanese creation would go on to become a global pop culture icon, symbolizing nuclear anxieties.

The Zoom Lens Debut

The introduction of the zoom lens in the 1950s allowed for dynamic shifts in focal lengths within a shot, creating new storytelling possibilities.

From Mono to Stereo

Transitioning from monophonic to stereophonic recordings, the '50s made movie soundtracks richer, enveloping audiences in immersive auditory experiences.

The Big Screen Experience

To compete with TV, Hollywood introduced widescreen formats like CinemaScope. Epics like "Ben-Hur" (1959) were perfect fits, offering grandeur TV couldn't match.

Brando's Method

Marlon Brando's method acting in "A Streetcar Named Desire" (1951) set new standards. His raw, emotive performance is still studied by actors today.

The End of an Era for Bogart

One of Hollywood's most iconic figures, Humphrey Bogart, passed away in 1957. His films, like "In a Lonely Place" (1950), remain testaments to his vast talent.

'50s Sci-Fi Fever

The decade's fascination with space and alien invasions was evident in movies. "The Day the Earth Stood Still" (1951) became a sci-fi classic, reflecting Cold War anxieties.

Doris Day's Shining Decade

Doris Day became one of the biggest stars of the '50s, showcasing her acting and singing talents in films like "Calamity Jane" (1953).

The Epic "Ben-Hur"

"Ben-Hur" (1959) wasn't just grand in story. With 11 Academy Awards, it tied for the most Oscars won by a single film—a record it still shares today.

CHAPTER

FIVE:

NEW WAVES
AND
GLOBAL CINEMA
(1960s)

THE '60s GLOBAL REVOLUTION

The 1960s were a decade of upheaval, not just in politics and society but vividly in the world of cinema. As the old Hollywood studio system began to crumble, fresh waves of filmmakers across the globe rose, crafting stories that would forever change the narrative of international cinema.

The camera, no longer confined to lavish sets or pristine studios, ventured onto the streets, into real homes, and amidst genuine crowds, capturing life in its rawest form.
From the bustling streets of Paris to the sweeping landscapes of Italy, from the intricate dance sequences of Bollywood to the intense martial arts duels of Hong Kong, cinema in the '60s was no longer just an escape—it was a reflection, a protest, a voice.

New techniques were not merely experimental but revolutionary, turning cinematic norms on their heads. The meticulous framing of Akira Kurosawa, the evocative long takes of Michelangelo Antonioni, and the boundary-pushing narratives of Jean-Luc Godard were all testimonies to an age where rules were meant to be broken.

In this chapter, cinema becomes the universal language of passion, resistance, and transformation, giving voice to a generation eager to tell its story.

The French Connection

The French New Wave, led by directors like Jean-Luc Godard and François Truffaut, redefined cinema with unconventional narratives and editing in classics like "Breathless" (1960).

Italian Realism's Evolution

Directors like Federico Fellini and Michelangelo Antonioni built upon Italian Neorealism's foundation, introducing more abstract and introspective films like "La Dolce Vita" (1960).

East Meets West

Japanese filmmaker Akira Kurosawa's "Yojimbo" (1961) influenced Western cinema, inspiring movies like Sergio Leone's "A Fistful of Dollars" (1964).

Bollywood's Golden Age

Indian cinema flourished with classics like "Mughal-e-Azam" (1960), a tale of love set against the backdrop of the Mughal Empire, setting new standards for grandeur.

The British Invasion

While the Beatles rocked the music scene, British cinema had its own revolution with gritty, realist films like "Saturday Night and Sunday Morning" (1960).

Rise of the Spaghetti Western

Italian directors, especially Sergio Leone, breathed new life into the Western genre, creating iconic films like "The Good, the Bad and the Ugly" (1966).

Czech Out the New Wave

The Czech New Wave brought innovative storytelling to the fore with films like "Closely Watched Trains" (1966), merging humor with social commentary.

The Wonders of Wide Shot

Films like David Lean's "Lawrence of Arabia" (1962) showcased the potential of 70mm film, capturing vast desert landscapes in breathtaking detail.

Brazilian Cinema's New Tide

The Brazilian Cinema Novo, inspired by neorealism and the French New Wave, aimed to reflect the country's socio-political landscape with films like "Black God, White Devil" (1964).

Hollywood Gets Experimental

Films like "Easy Rider" (1969) broke traditional narrative molds, heralding a new era of experimental and countercultural filmmaking in Hollywood.

African Cinema Awakens

Senegal's Ousmane Sembène, considered the father of African cinema, released "Black Girl" (1966), a poignant tale of a Senegalese maid in France.

The Color of Music

"Yellow Submarine" (1968) wasn't just a Beatles musical trip—it was a vivid explosion of animation techniques and psychedelic art.

A Space Odyssey

Stanley Kubrick's "2001: A Space Odyssey" (1968) was revolutionary, showcasing unparalleled special effects and redefining sci-fi cinema.

Chinese Martial Arts Take Flight

The 1960s saw the rise of martial arts films from Hong Kong, with stars like Bruce Lee captivating audiences with gravity-defying stunts.

Revolution in the Air

Political unrest globally influenced cinema. Films like Gillo Pontecorvo's "The Battle of Algiers" (1966) provided harrowing looks at colonial struggles and uprisings.

CHAPTER

SIX:

BLOCKBUSTERS
AND
NEW HOLLYWOOD
(1970s)

Hollywood's Game-Changing Decade

If cinema had a revolution, the 1970s would undoubtedly be its epicenter. This was the decade when film conventions were not just challenged but dramatically overhauled, as the edgy, avant-garde visions of New Hollywood directors met the phenomenon of blockbusters, crafting a form of storytelling that still influences the movies we watch today.

The old guard of studio-system Hollywood had given way to a new breed of filmmakers. These young mavericks, armed with fresh perspectives and audacious creativity, sought to tell raw, unfiltered stories. They delved deep into the American psyche, exploring its dreams and nightmares, its heroes and antiheroes.

Martin Scorsese's urban desolation, Francis Ford Coppola's operatic gangster tales, and Steven Spielberg's masterful blend of wonder and terror—all painted a multifaceted portrait of a society in flux.

Yet, it wasn't just about introspective narratives. The 70s saw the birth of the blockbuster, a cultural and commercial juggernaut that would define modern cinematic experiences. From the ominous strains of the "Jaws" theme to the iconic crawl of "Star Wars," these movies were larger than life, events that drew audiences into theaters in droves, transforming cinema into a collective, communal celebration.

Hollywood's Game-Changing Decade

The disco-drenched dance floors, the chilling corridors of haunted homes, the political corridors of Washington, and the far reaches of interstellar space—cinema in the 70s was a sprawling, vivid tapestry that refused to be boxed into genres or conventions.

A time when movies became more than just entertainment—they were reflections, reactions, and often revolutions, shaping not just the film industry but the cultural zeitgeist of a generation.

Birth of the Blockbuster

Steven Spielberg's "Jaws" (1975) wasn't just a thrilling shark tale; it introduced the summer blockbuster, changing movie marketing and distribution forever.

The Force Awakens

George Lucas's "Star Wars" (1977) blended science fiction with epic mythology, creating an intergalactic phenomenon and forever altering the landscape of franchise films.

A Gritty New York

Martin Scorsese's "Taxi Driver" (1976) portrayed New York's grimy underbelly with Robert De Niro's chilling line, "You talkin' to me?" forever echoing in cinematic history.

Rise of the Antihero

The '70s celebrated flawed characters, with films like "One Flew Over the Cuckoo's Nest" (1975) showcasing Jack Nicholson's nuanced portrayal of rebellion against oppression.

Horror Takes a Leap

"The Exorcist" (1973) terrified audiences around the world, becoming one of the most successful and influential horror films of all time.

Epic Storytelling

Francis Ford Coppola's "The Godfather" (1972) wasn't just a mob movie; it was a poetic saga of power, family, and the American dream, earning universal acclaim.

Sound of Revolution

George Lucas's sound company, THX, was founded in 1983, but the groundwork began in the '70s, enhancing cinematic soundscapes and transforming audio experiences in theaters.

Animated Renaissance Begins

Though Disney faced challenges, "The Rescuers" (1977) signaled hope, setting the stage for the company's resurgence in the next decade.

Women Behind the Camera

Director Barbara Loden broke new ground with "Wanda" (1970), hailed as one of the first feminist feature films directed by a woman.

Cult Classics Flourish

"The Rocky Horror Picture Show" (1975) may have had a rocky start, but it evolved into a beloved midnight movie, with audiences engaging in lively theater rituals.

Indies Enter the Scene

John Cassavetes's "A Woman Under the Influence" (1974) exemplified the rise of independent cinema, focusing on deep character studies and raw emotion.

Apocalypse on Screen

"Apocalypse Now" (1979) wasn't just about the Vietnam War; it was an exploration of humanity's heart of darkness, blending realism with surreal imagery.

Disco and Dance

"Saturday Night Fever" (1977) wasn't just a film; it was a cultural phenomenon, propelling John Travolta to stardom and making disco an enduring symbol of the '70s.

A Galaxy of Special Effects

Industrial Light & Magic (ILM), founded in 1975 by George Lucas, transformed visual effects, creating magical moments in movies like "Close Encounters of the Third Kind" (1977).

Real Stories, Raw Cinema

Films like "All the President's Men" (1976) captured the essence of true events, bringing journalistic intrigue to the big screen and emphasizing cinema's role in reflecting societal issues.

CHAPTER

SEVEN:

THE AGE
OF
FRANCHISES
AND
SPECIAL EFFECTS
(1980s)

BLOCKBUSTERS AND BEYOND

The 1980s wasn't just about big hair, neon lights, and synth beats; it was a decade where cinema took a bold leap into the realm of the extraordinary.

Hollywood, with its fingers on the pulsating heart of technology and an eye on box-office gold, recognized the era's potential, creating films that would forever redefine the way we experienced stories on the big screen.

Imagine a time when film enthusiasts, armed with buckets of popcorn, sat wide-eyed as they witnessed a young archaeologist outrun a boulder, or a teenager zip through time in a car powered by a flux capacitor. This was a decade where the boundaries between reality and fiction blurred, allowing audiences to be transported from the grim, rain-soaked streets of a dystopian future in "Blade Runner" to the whimsical and perilous maze of "Labyrinth."

It wasn't just the stories that evolved; it was how they were told. The advancements in special effects and CGI were no less than a cinematic revolution. From the hauntingly beautiful digital world of "Tron" to the practical effects that breathed life into E.T. or the monstrous Thing, filmmakers were crafting visual wonders, making the impossible seem palpably real.
But, while the visual spectacle grew, it wasn't at the expense of heart.

BLOCKBUSTERS AND BEYOND

Films like "E.T. the Extra-Terrestrial" or "Back to the Future" reminded us that, at the core of every great film, lay relatable human emotions and connections.

The '80s were also the breeding ground for franchises.
Star Wars expanded its galactic reach, Indiana Jones whipped his way into cinematic legend, and new series like "Die Hard" and "The Terminator" ensured that Hollywood's commercial potential was fully realized.

Welcome to the Digital Age

The 1982 film "Tron" was groundbreaking, not just for its story, but for being one of the first films to use extensive computer-generated imagery, ushering in a digital era in cinema.

E.T. Phones Home...

Steven Spielberg's "E.T. the Extra-Terrestrial" (1982) captured hearts worldwide, becoming an instant classic and showcasing the magic of practical effects paired with heartfelt storytelling.

The Force Expands

George Lucas continued the "Star Wars" saga with "The Empire Strikes Back" (1980) and "Return of the Jedi" (1983), deepening the lore and pushing the boundaries of special effects.

Raiders of the Lost Franchise

The debut of "Indiana Jones" in "Raiders of the Lost Ark" (1981) by Spielberg and Lucas marked the birth of another legendary film series, with an adventurous archeologist at its core.

Welcome to the Terrordome

John Carpenter's "The Thing" (1982) may have had a chilly reception initially, but its revolutionary practical effects and tense storytelling made it a horror hallmark.

The Rise of the Robots

James Cameron's "The Terminator" (1984) introduced a relentless cyborg from the future, blending sci-fi and action in a way that set the stage for many films to come.

A Ghastly Gang's Debut

"Ghostbusters" (1984) combined comedy, special effects, and the supernatural, creating an iconic franchise that resonated with both kids and adults.

Dance, Magic, Dance!

Jim Henson's puppet mastery shone in "Labyrinth" (1986), a fantastical journey featuring David Bowie and a maze of memorable characters.

Predators and Aliens

The 1980s gave sci-fi fans both "Predator" (1987) and the continuation of Ridley Scott's "Alien" series with "Aliens" (1986), showcasing creature effects at their finest.

An Unexpected Journey in Time

"Back to the Future" (1985) was more than a DeLorean's joyride. It crafted a time-traveling tale for the ages, launching a beloved trilogy.

Adventure in Animation

Disney's "The Little Mermaid" (1989) signaled the start of the animation renaissance, with its catchy tunes and vibrant underwater world.

Fears from the TV Screen

"Poltergeist" (1982), co-written and produced by Spielberg, warned of the eerie happenings that surround a suburban family's TV set, blending the mundane with the supernatural.

Nakatomi Plaza Showdown

"Die Hard" (1988) with Bruce Willis didn't just give us memorable catchphrases; it redefined the action film genre and gave birth to a franchise.

New Dimensions in Horror

Clive Barker's "Hellraiser" (1987) introduced the world to Pinhead and the Cenobites, pushing the boundaries of horror imagery and practical effects.

A Game of Cat and Mouse

"Who Framed Roger Rabbit" (1988) was a unique blend of live-action and animation, seamlessly bringing cartoon characters into the real world and setting a new bar for visual integration.

CHAPTER

EIGHT:

DIGITAL REVOLUTION

AND

INDIE FILMS

(1990s)

Pixelated Visions & Indie Passions

As the neon haze of the '80s dimmed, the 1990s dawned with an electrifying promise—a synthesis of technological advancement and the emergence of new, audacious voices that would reshape the contours of cinema.

The '90s wasn't just a decade; it was a cinematic renaissance where the lines between blockbuster extravaganzas and indie darlings began to blur, creating a mosaic of stories that catered to every palate.

In one corner, there were the titans of technology, pushing pixels to their limit. When the majestic roar of a T-Rex from "Jurassic Park" reverberated through cinema halls, audiences worldwide realized they weren't just watching a movie; they were witnessing a revolution. Digital creatures, once confined to our imaginations, now roamed the silver screen, lifelike and awe-inspiring.

Yet, while digital wizards conjured fantastical worlds, independent auteurs, armed with shoestring budgets and unbridled passion, painted poignant tales. Movies like "Pulp Fiction" and "Clerks" weren't just films; they were statements, a clarion call to mainstream cinema, proclaiming that you didn't need million-dollar budgets to captivate audiences.

Pixelated Visions & Indie Passions

These were stories raw, unfiltered, and radically different from the norm.

Even as films like "The Matrix" plunged audiences into synthetic realities, indie films reminded us of the humbling and often chaotic tapestry of human emotions. They might not have had the glitz of CGI, but they glittered with genuine, heartfelt narratives.

Furthermore, the decade was also about accessibility. The birth of Netflix, initially a humble DVD-by-mail service, hinted at the dawn of a new era where cinema would be democratized, reaching viewers in the cozy comfort of their homes.

Digital Dinosaurs

Steven Spielberg's "Jurassic Park" (1993) was a milestone, using cutting-edge CGI to bring life-sized dinosaurs to the big screen, redefining visual effects in cinema.

Indie Darling Takes the Gold

Quentin Tarantino's "Pulp Fiction" (1994) blended non-linear storytelling, sharp dialogue, and eclectic soundtracks, becoming a beacon for indie filmmakers and snagging the Palme d'Or at Cannes.

To Infinity and Beyond

"Toy Story" (1995) wasn't just a tale of toys coming to life. As Pixar's first full-length feature, it was the world's first entirely computer-animated film.

The Resurgence of a Galaxy Far, Far Away

George Lucas tapped into the power of digital technology, releasing the Star Wars Special Editions and introducing the prequel trilogy starting with "The Phantom Menace" (1999).

The Blair Witch Phenomenon

"The Blair Witch Project" (1999) was indie filmmaking at its peak. Shot on a shoestring budget, its viral marketing campaign made it a massive hit, popularizing the found-footage genre.

A Trip Down the Rabbit Hole

"The Matrix" (1999) combined dazzling visual effects with a thought-provoking narrative, introducing 'bullet-time' cinematography and sparking discussions on reality and AI.

Birth of a Digital Distribution Giant

1997 saw the launch of Netflix, initially as a DVD-by-mail service. It would later pivot to streaming, forever changing how we consume content.

A Sundance Fairy Tale

Kevin Smith's "Clerks" (1994), made on a tight budget, showcased the potential of indie films when it became a critical and commercial success after premiering at the Sundance Film Festival.

Mafioso Magic on the Small Screen

While cinema soared, television also saw gems. "The Sopranos" debuted in 1999, heralding a new age of cinematic quality for TV dramas.

Ghibli Garners Global Gaze

Hayao Miyazaki's "Princess Mononoke" (1997) broke box office records in Japan and garnered global attention, spotlighting Studio Ghibli's animation prowess.

The Rebirth of the Romantic Comedy

Nora Ephron's "You've Got Mail" (1998) combined classic romantic charm with the modern age of the internet, reinventing the rom-com for a new era.

A Masterpiece from the East

"Chungking Express" (1994) by Wong Kar-wai brought the vivid, neon-lit streets of Hong Kong to international audiences, signifying the global reach of indie films.

Founding of a Film Titan

DreamWorks SKG was founded in 1994 by Steven Spielberg, Jeffrey Katzenberg, and David Geffen, aiming to combine film, music, and television into a powerful entertainment entity.

A Noir-Style Modern Classic

The Coen Brothers' "Fargo" (1996) with its quirky characters, dark humor, and snowy landscapes demonstrated that indie films could offer unique narratives and earn mainstream acclaim.

From the Ashes Rises the Phoenix

After some financial struggles, Marvel formed Marvel Studios in 1996, a decision that would eventually lead to the superhero cinema explosion in the 21st century.

CHAPTER

NINE:

THE AGE

OF

SUPERHEROES

AND

STREAMING

(2000s - 2010s)

Capes, Clicks, & Cinematic Evolution

As the clock ticked towards the new millennium, a cinematic wave was on the horizon—a wave that would be characterized by larger-than-life superheroes, digital escapades, and a seismic shift in how we consumed content.

The 2000s and 2010s weren't just decades; they were transformative eras where cinema and technology danced a passionate tango.

Enter the superheroes. Caped crusaders and masked vigilantes who once graced the pages of comic books took flight on the silver screen, redefining blockbuster cinema.

Whether it was Tony Stark suiting up as Iron Man, or the dark, enigmatic world of Gotham under the shadow of the Bat, superheroes became modern myths, embodying our hopes, fears, and aspirations.

But while the theaters resonated with the sounds of clashing shields and thundering Mjölnirs, a quieter revolution was simmering at home. With a simple click, viewers could dive into vast oceans of content. Netflix, once a humble DVD delivery service, redefined binge-watching, leading the vanguard of streaming platforms that transformed our living rooms into personal theaters.

Capes, Clicks, & Cinematic Evolution

This era wasn't just about the grandeur of superheroes or the convenience of streaming; it was also an epoch that celebrated diverse voices.

Indie filmmakers from every corner of the globe found platforms and audiences, challenging norms and crafting narratives that were as compelling as they were unique. From the bustling streets of Mumbai in "Slumdog Millionaire" to the deceptive serenity of a South Korean home in "Parasite," cinema became a global conversation.

The Billion-Dollar Marvel

The release of "Iron Man" in 2008 not only introduced Tony Stark to audiences but also kicked off the Marvel Cinematic Universe (MCU), a mega-franchise that would dominate the box office for years to come.

Streaming Becomes Mainstream

Netflix, initially a DVD rental service, pivoted to streaming in 2007, forever changing the way we binge-watch our favorite shows and movies.

Gotham's Dark Knight Rises

Christopher Nolan's "The Dark Knight" (2008) transcended the superhero genre, delivering a gritty and cerebral exploration of justice and chaos, with Heath Ledger's portrayal of the Joker becoming legendary.

Avatar's Alien World

James Cameron's "Avatar" (2009) set a new standard for CGI, creating the vibrant world of Pandora, and held the title of the highest-grossing film for a decade.

Waking the Wizarding World

The new millennium saw the rise of the "Harry Potter" film series (2001-2011), enchanting muggles worldwide and introducing them to the magical world of Hogwarts.

Binge-Worthy Epics

"Game of Thrones," premiering in 2011 on HBO, showcased the potential of TV series to rival big-screen epics in terms of scale, storytelling, and character development.

A Digital Oscars Victory

Pixar's "Up" (2009) became the first ever animated film to open the Cannes Film Festival and the second animated film to receive a Best Picture Oscar nomination.

The Reign of Streaming Giants

The 2010s witnessed the rise of streaming giants like Amazon Prime and Hulu, with platforms creating original content and revolutionizing the industry's landscape.

The Superheroine's Stand

"Patty Jenkins' "Wonder Woman" (2017) broke multiple records, proving that superheroines could stand tall at the box office and inspiring a generation.

Indie Gems Shine Bright

"Slumdog Millionaire" (2008), an indie film with a modest budget, swept the Oscars and became a global sensation, highlighting the power of unconventional narratives.

From Books to Big Screen

"The Hunger Games" trilogy (2012-2015) set the box office ablaze, underlining the 2000s trend of adapting young adult novels into successful film franchises.

An Oscars Underdog Triumph

Bong Joon-ho's "Parasite" (2019), a South Korean dark comedy thriller, made history as the first non-English language film to win the Best Picture Oscar.

Reviving Nostalgia

"Stranger Things" (2016), a Netflix original, took audiences on a nostalgic trip to the '80s, combining supernatural elements with a heartwarming tale of friendship.

A Universe Beyond Marvel

DC, not to be outdone, launched its own Extended Universe (DCEU) with "Man of Steel" in 2013, expanding the superhero battles to new frontiers.

The Galactic Saga Continues

The 2000s saw the return of "Star Wars" with both prequels and sequels, as George Lucas and later Disney continued the legacy of the galaxy far, far away.

CHAPTER TEN:

NEW HORIZONS: VR, AR, AND BEYOND (2020s AND BEYOND)

The Theoretical Tapestry of Tomorrow's Cinema

The story of cinema is a narrative interwoven with innovation. From the flickering shadows of the Lumière brothers' early moving pictures to the jaw-dropping 3D visuals of our contemporary blockbusters, every era has pushed the boundaries of what's possible, both in technology and storytelling. Yet, as we stand on the precipice of what might be cinema's most transformative era yet, it's essential to remember that much of what we envision is speculative, steeped in the realm of possibility rather than certainty.

The 2020s and beyond present us with a tantalizing array of potential futures. We dream of virtual realities where stories envelop us, augmented realms where fiction seamlessly blends with our physical world, and artificial intelligences that might soon pen scripts as poignant as any human. The line between viewer and participant, reality and fiction, could become as blurred as it is beguiling.

Yet, for all these futuristic forecasts, there's an inherent magic in traditional cinema—a shared experience in a darkened theater, the collective gasp of an audience at a plot twist, or the emotive power of a close-up on a giant screen. The essence of film, the shared experience of storytelling, remains a constant, even as the mediums and methods evolve.

The Theoretical Tapestry of Tomorrow's Cinema

It's worth noting that while these new horizons are undeniably exciting, they're still theories. Predicting the future is a gamble, and as history often reminds us, the next big thing in cinema might be something entirely unexpected, an innovation or trend no one saw coming. Perhaps, as we dream of AR landscapes and VR narratives, the future might also see a renaissance of retro—a resurgence of the tangible, the analog, the organic.

In exploring the possibilities of tomorrow's cinema, we should cherish the legacies of yesteryears and today. For no matter how advanced our tech becomes or how immersive our movie experiences might be, the heart of cinema—a good story, well-told—will likely always find its most resonant home in the traditional flicker of the projector's light.

Cinematic Realities

By the early 2020s, virtual reality (VR) cinemas started emerging, offering audiences a fully immersive 360-degree movie-watching experience, redefining the boundaries between viewer and story.

Augmented Actors

Using augmented reality (AR), filmmakers began overlaying digital enhancements in real-world settings, making every location a potential movie set.

A New Dimension of Horror

Horror films, always at the forefront of utilizing new techniques, quickly embraced VR to deliver chills, placing viewers directly into the heart of their darkest fears.

Holographic Premieres

Hollywood premieres saw a futuristic twist with stars attending as holograms, ensuring they could "walk" any red carpet worldwide without leaving home.

AI Directors

The first films directed with the assistance of artificial intelligence algorithms emerged, suggesting plot twists and camera angles based on audience data.

Crowd-Powered Plotlines

Interactive cinema reached new heights, with audiences voting in real-time via AR glasses to choose plot directions, leading to multiple story outcomes in a single screening.

Reality Blends with Fiction

Using AR, locations from popular films became tourist attractions, allowing fans to see movie scenes overlaid onto real-world settings through AR glasses.

Personalized Soundscapes

Films began offering customizable soundtracks, using AI to adjust music and sound effects in real-time based on individual viewer emotions.

The Return of Silent Cinema

In an unexpected twist, a trend of modern silent films emerged, using VR and AR to focus on visual storytelling without spoken dialogue.

From Seats to Scenes

Traditional cinema halls underwent transformational redesigns, moving from fixed seating to interactive spaces where viewers could walk around during VR films.

Immersive Adaptations

Classic films were reimagined for VR, allowing viewers to step directly into iconic scenes and interact with beloved characters.

Virtual Film Festivals

Popular film festivals like Cannes and Sundance created virtual editions, allowing attendees to experience film debuts from the comfort of their VR headsets.

Emotional Feedback Loops

Advanced biometric systems in VR headsets gauged viewer emotions, adjusting film pacing and mood in response to real-time reactions.

Cinematic Videogames

The line between movies and video games blurred further as AAA game titles adopted movie-length narratives and character arcs, making players both viewers and protagonists.

Echoes of the Past

With the advent of deepfake technology and holography, iconic actors of yesteryears made "comebacks" in new films.

A Standing Ovation Just For You!

Dear Reader,

As the credits roll, I want to take a moment to spotlight the most important character in this story - you, the reader.

Your decision to read this book, whether during a moment of respite in your restroom retreats or as a curious explorer of film facts, is the reason these pages came to life.

Movies, much like books, are about connecting with an audience. And just as every film hopes to leave a mark on its viewer, my aspiration was to offer you a blend of entertainment and enlightenment, one tidbit at a time.

I hope you left with a smile, perhaps a newfound piece of trivia to share at your next gathering, and most importantly, a deeper appreciation for the magic of cinema.

As they say in the movies, "The End." But in the world of readers and storytellers, every end is just a new beginning. Here's to many more tales, shared moments, and delightful discoveries. 🎬

Thank You,

Herman Cooper

ALSO AVAILABLE

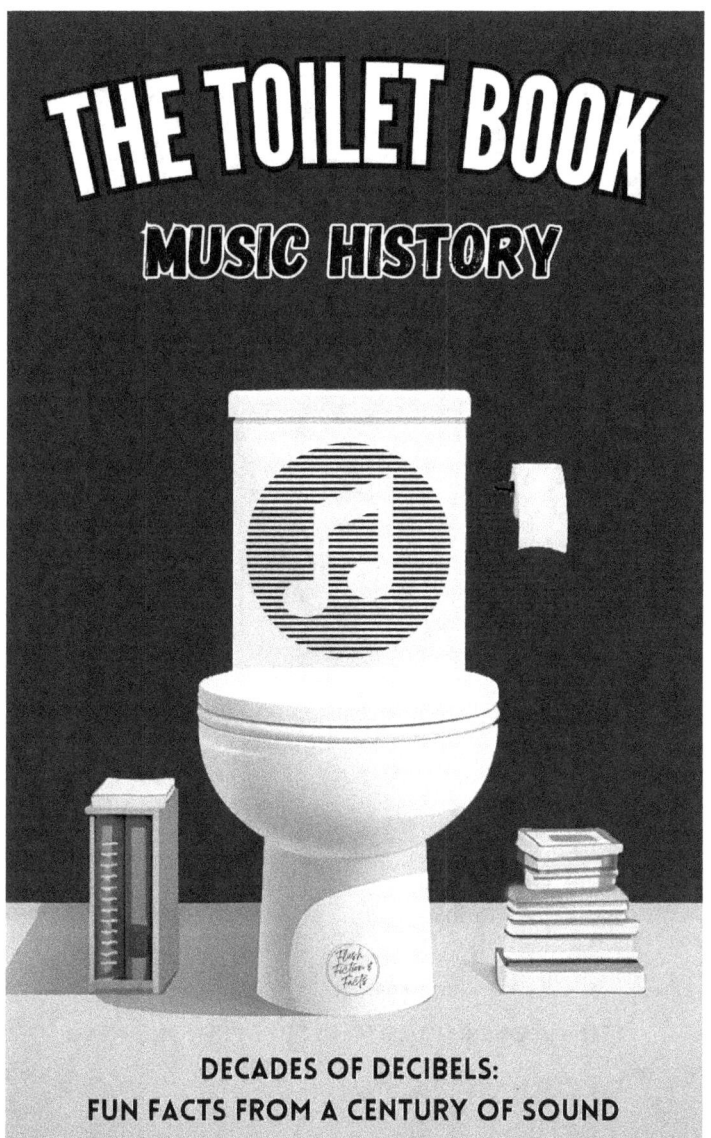

THE TOILET BOOK

MUSIC HISTORY

DECADES OF DECIBELS:
FUN FACTS FROM A CENTURY OF SOUND

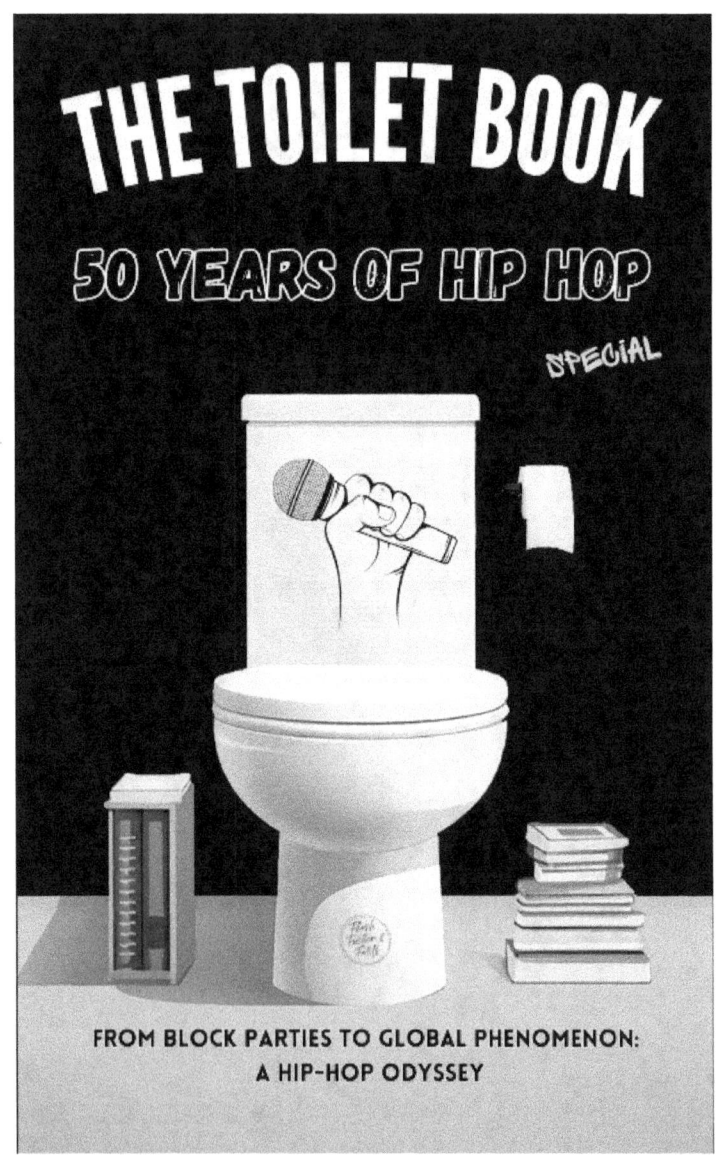

Coming Soon

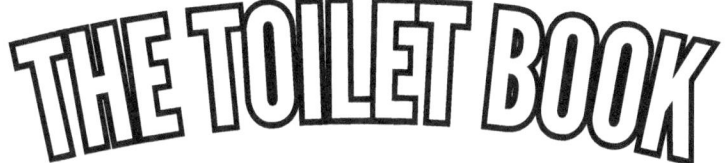

Beer
American Sports
World Sports
Video Games
Halloween
Thanksgiving
Christmas
Basketball History
Wine
American History
Football History

and many more...

www.thetoiletbooks.com

www.ingramcontent.com/pod-product-compliance
Lightning Source LLC
Chambersburg PA
CBHW072337290526
45794CB00002B/917